D0842582

Your Favorite Authors

JACQUELINE WOODSON

by Lisa M. Bolt Simons

CAPSTONE PRESS
a capstone imprint

First Facts are published by Capstone Press,
1710 Roe Crest Drive, North Mankato, Minnesota 56003
www.mycapstone.com

Library of Congress Cataloging-in-Publication Data
Names: Simons, Lisa M. B., 1969– author.
Title: Jacqueline Woodson / By Lisa M. Bolt Simons.
Description: North Mankato, Minnesota : First Facts, 2017. | Series: First facts.
Your favorite authors. | Includes bibliographical references.
Identifiers: LCCN 2016023234| ISBN 9781515735588 (library binding) |
ISBN 9781515735632 (pbk.) | ISBN 9781515735670 (ebook (pdf)
Subjects: LCSH: Woodson, Jacqueline—Juvenile literature. | Authors, American—20th
century—Biography—Juvenile literature.
Classification: LCC PS3573.O64524 Z84 2017 | DDC 813/.54 [B]—dc23
LC record available at https://lccn.loc.gov/2016023234

Editorial Credits
Carrie Braulick Sheely and Michelle Hasselius, editors; Kayla Dohmen, designer;
Ruth Smith, media researcher; Gene Bentdahl, production specialist

Photo Credits
Alamy Images: Jonny White, 9; Associated Press: MARK LENNIHAN, 17;
Capstone Press: Michael Byers, cover, 15; Getty Images: AFP, 8, Hulton Archive, 9, Robin
Marchant, 5, 19, Rommel Demano, 21; Shutterstock: Apostrophe, cover, balabolka, cover,
background design elements, Bruce Stanfield, 7 BR, Cvandyke, 7 BL, Cynthia Kidwell,
7 M, goir, 7 TM, Graphic design, 7 TR, Milan M, 7 TL, photo.ua, 13, Victor Moussa, 13,
wavebreakmedia, 11, 21

Printed in the United States of America.
092016   010030S17

Table of Contents

Chapter 1: Changing the World

In 2014 Jacqueline Woodson was a finalist for a major award. It was the third time she was up to win the National Book Award in Young People's Literature. At the ceremony Woodson won! The award honored her **memoir** *Brown Girl Dreaming*. In her speech she said, "Thank you for your love of books. And thank you for changing the world." It was a proud moment in her long career as a writer.

---

memoir—a story from one's life

Woodson at the 2014 National Book Awards

Chapter 2: Watching Words Flower

Jacqueline Woodson was born on February 12, 1963, in Columbus, Ohio. Her family then moved to Greenville, South Carolina. When she was 3 years old, her sister taught her how to write her name. Woodson said she soon "fell in love" with letters and making words.

Woodson's family moved to Brooklyn, New York, when she was 7 years old. She wrote whenever and wherever she could. Once her uncle even caught her writing **graffiti** on a building.

---

graffiti—pictures drawn or words written with spray paint on buildings, bridges, and trains; most graffiti is illegal

"I loved and still love watching words flower into sentences and sentences blossom into stories."—Jacqueline Woodson

Columbus, Ohio

Welcome to Greenville

In elementary school Woodson wrote a poem about Martin Luther King, Jr. At first few people believed she wrote it, because it was so good. Woodson wrote her first story in 5th grade. She remembers her teacher smiled and said that the story was really good. These early successes helped Woodson become **confident**.

Civil Rights Leader Martin Luther King, Jr.

---

confident—having a strong belief in your own abilities

Learning Poetry

Woodson read work from Poet Langston Hughes in school. His poems helped her understand and love poetry. She memorized his poem "Dreams." The poem appears in the beginning of *Brown Girl Dreaming*.

Langston Hughes

Woodson sometimes struggled in school. She once took the same math class three times. Reading was not easy for her. But books were a big part of her life. Woodson and her siblings often visited the local library. She worked hard to improve.

After high school Woodson went to Adelphi University in New York. She studied English and British **literature**.

---

literature—written works that have lasting value or interest

"I used to say I'd be a teacher or a lawyer or a hairdresser when I grew up, but even as I said these things, I knew what made me happiest was writing."—Jacqueline Woodson

Chapter 3: Windows, Mirrors, and Awards

Woodson read all kinds of books. She felt some books were "windows" that showed how others lived. Woodson wanted books that were "mirrors." These books would reflect her life.

Woodson started writing her first **novel** in college. It was about African-American girls. The girls grew up in Brooklyn like her. The book came out in 1990. It was the first book of a **trilogy**.

---

novel—prose or narrative that is not true; a long fictional book

trilogy—a set of three works, such as books

Brooklyn, New York

In 1995 Woodson's novel *I Hadn't Meant to Tell You This* won a Coretta Scott King Author Honor. The story is about two girls who don't have moms and become friends.

In 2001 Woodson won the Coretta Scott King Award for *Miracle's Boys*. There are no girl characters in the story. Woodson wanted to try writing a book about a family that had only boys.

Each Book In Its Own Time

Woodson wrote one of her books in two weeks. It didn't need a lot of revisions. But her next book took four years to write!

Woodson continued to get praise for her books over the next several years.

Woodson's novel *Hush* was **published** in 2002. It was a finalist for the National Book Award. The next year her novel *Locomotion* was a finalist for the same award. Her picture book *Coming on Home Soon* won a Caldecott Honor in 2005. This book is about a young African-American girl. The girl struggles with **loneliness** after her mother goes to work during World War II (1939–1945).

---

publish—to produce and distribute a book, magazine, newspaper, or any other printed material so that people can buy it

loneliness—sadness because you are by yourself

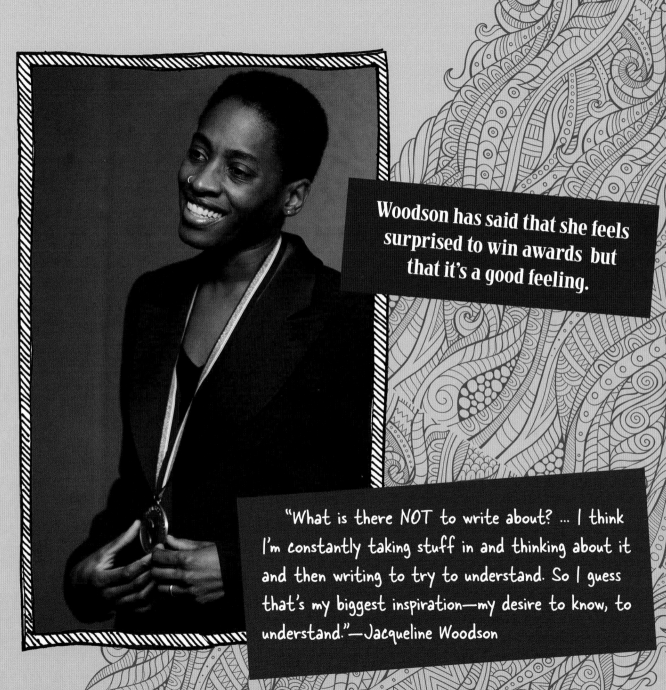

Woodson has said that she feels surprised to win awards but that it's a good feeling.

"What is there NOT to write about? ... I think I'm constantly taking stuff in and thinking about it and then writing to try to understand. So I guess that's my biggest inspiration—my desire to know, to understand."—Jacqueline Woodson

Woodson writes books for all ages. She believes she's writing for people "across the **generations**."

Woodson continues to win awards for her work. She's received the Newbery Honor four times. This award is for American books that are considered the best for children. *Brown Girl Dreaming* earned a Newbery Honor in 2015.

---

generation—a group of people born around the same time

Brown Girl Dreaming has earned Woodson several honors and awards.

Chapter 4: Poet Laureate

Woodson has published more than 25 books. In 2015 she became the Young People's Poet **Laureate**. In this role Woodson helps children learn to love poetry. She believes young people should have books to read and stories to tell.

---

laureate—a person recognized for an achievement

Woodson attends the Moving Families Forward Gala in New York City in 2015. The event raised money for family therapy services.

"Even when the words are slow in coming and the story seems all lopsided, writing keeps me happy."—Jacqueline Woodson

Timeline

1963	born in Columbus, Ohio
1990	first book is published, *Last Summer with Maizon*
2000	wins *Los Angeles Times* Book Prize for *Miracle's Boys*
2001	wins Coretta Scott King Author Award for *Miracle's Boys*
2002	becomes National Book Award Finalist for *Hush*
2003	becomes National Book Award Finalist for *Locomotion*
2006	wins Margaret A. Edwards Award for lifetime achievement
2008	wins Newbery Honor for *Feathers*
2014	is finalist for Hans Christian Andersen Award Shortlist, an international award
2014	wins National Book Award in Young People's Literature for *Brown Girl Dreaming*
2015	wins Coretta Scott King Author Award for *Brown Girl Dreaming*
2015	wins Newbery Honor for *Brown Girl Dreaming*
2015	is chosen as the Young People's Poet Laureate

Glossary

confident (KON-fi-duhnt)—having a strong belief in your own abilities

generation (jen-uh-RAY-shuhn)—a group of people born around the same time

graffiti (gruh-FEE-tee)—pictures drawn or words written with spray paint on buildings, bridges, and trains; most graffiti is illegal

laureate (LOR-ee-uht)—a person recognized for an achievement

literature (LIT-ur-uh-chur)—written works that have lasting value or interest

loneliness (LONE-lee-nes)—sadness because you are by yourself

memoir (MEM-wohr)—a story from one's life

novel (NOV-uhl)—prose or narrative that is not true; a long fictional book

publish (PUHB-lish)—to produce and distribute a book, magazine, newspaper, or any other printed material so that people can buy it

trilogy (TRILL-uh-jee)—a set of three works, such as books

Read More

Shelton, Paula Young. *Child of the Civil Rights Movement.* New York: Schwartz & Wade Books, 2010.

Sullivan, Laura Lee. *Jacqueline Woodson.* New York: Cavendish Square Publishing, 2015.

Internet Sites

FactHound offers a safe, fun way to find Internet sites related to this book. All of the sites on FactHound have been researched by our staff.

Here's all you do:

Visit *www.facthound.com*

Type in this code: 9781515735588

Index

Super-cool stuff!

Check out projects, games and lots more at
www.capstonekids.com